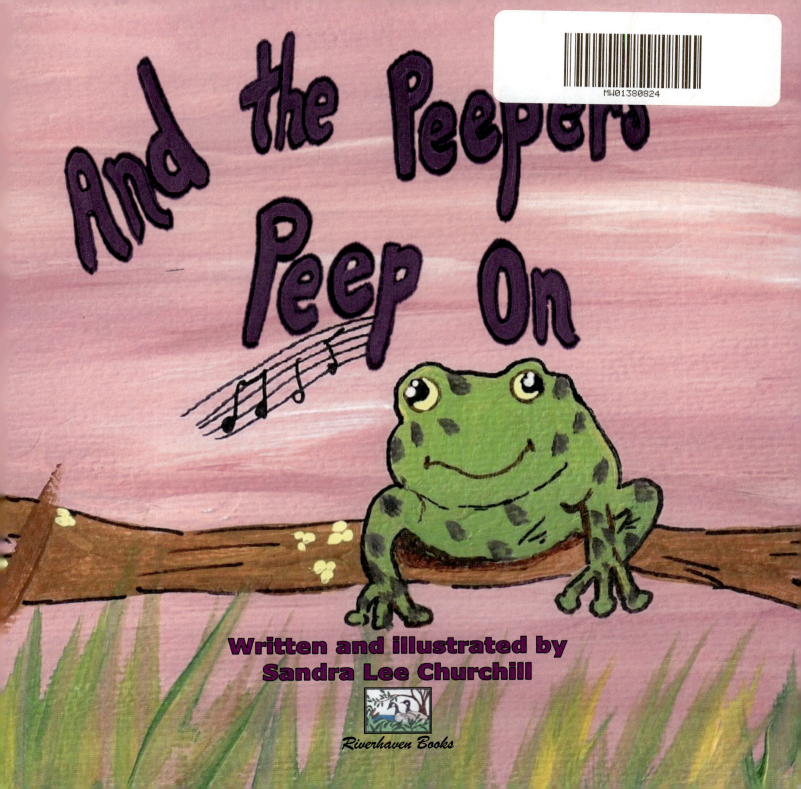

And the Peepers Peep On is a work of fiction intended to provide readers with a sense of normalcy.

Copyright© 2020 by Sandra Lee Churchill
All rights reserved.

Published in the United States by Riverhaven Books, www.RiverhavenBooks.com

ISBN : 978-1-951854-07-2

Printed in the United States of America

Designed and Edited by Stephanie Lynn Blackman
Whitman, MA

This book is dedicated to all the families out there navigating tough quarantines and unprecedented circumstances with COVID-19, as well as those managing life stresses when things don't go as planned.

Heartfelt gratitude to two "Stephanies" – my lovely editor-aficionado daughter and my talented publisher. Thank you to my supportive husband, Mark, and wonderfully creative Brittany, Timothy, Andy, and Tim L. who listened, suggested, and – through it all – loved!

With prayers and "social-distance" hugs
and love in good times and in bad!

SLC

We have new rules to follow now
To keep our loved ones safe.
Some things will change a bit or more,
But lots will stay the same.

Although we know we can't go out
And need to stay right here,
If we embrace the gifts we have,
What's good is always near.

All sports are canceled for a while,
We have no school for days,
Piano lessons, parties gone...
No friends can come to play...

And Mommy stays at home now too.
She's busy on Zoom meet.

The news keeps coming day and night,
With worried grownup talk.
We take a break as twilight nears
For after-dinner walks.

Soon nighttime comes, it's time for bed
I wish and wonder when
All work and games and party fun
Will be the same again.

I snuggle down, keep very still,
In cozy covers deep,
I listen for the peepers now,
They're singing me to sleep.

Made in the USA
Middletown, DE
19 June 2020